Jari Niemi

The Best Leader

Publisher: BoD · Books on Demand GmbH, Helsinki, Finland

Print: Libri Plureos GmbH, Hamburg, Germany

ISBN: 978-952-80-8262-0

AI has been used in the process of translating this book.

Contents

Dedicated to all current and new leaders.

Throughout my career, I've always embraced the opportunity to share knowledge, expertise, and innovative ideas. I've never viewed it as a loss to share successful methods and practices to others. Instead, it's been incredibly fulfilling to contribute to the growth and advancement of fellow professionals. This ethos of openness underpins the writing of this book. I sincerely hope it sparks valuable insights and ideas for your own leadership journey.

Over the years, I've frequently been asked about my guiding principles in leadership. I've willingly mentored and coached those eager to learn. Witnessing their development has been immensely gratifying. Each interaction has not only contributed to the growth of others but has also enriched my own leadership skills.

In this book, I've tried to seal my core thoughts on leadership and touch upon various related subjects. I would greatly appreciate your feedback on the book — positive comments on X or LinkedIn using the hashtag **#thebestleader**, and constructive criticism via email at **parasjohtaja@gmail.com**.

Foreword

Who is the world's best leader? Personally, I see the question's absolute answer as irrelevant: it doesn't matter. Unfortunately, you won't find the answer in this book, but you might discover something more important: the goal and the means.

Consider a retiree reflecting on her/his career and the leaders encountered along the way. Who was the best among them? Who was the worst? Whom would she/he absolutely never want to meet again? And why? It is likely that there were many leaders in total. Some were remembered only vaguely — the "neutral" ones. Only the best and the worst stand out in the memory. Several "average leaders" may not be remembered at all. The question is: Do you want to be remembered?

At the very least, you don't want to be remembered as a poor leader. Don't we all aspire to be good supervisors? It requires investing in both your team and yourself. Unfortunately, the path won't be entirely smooth.

However, I believe that just being "good" is not enough in this matter. Why set the goal modestly when you could strive to be the best? Isn't it worthwhile to set the bar high from the start and be the leader all your team members remember as the best in their career?

Here, "the best" doesn't arrogantly mean "the world's best" in comparison to others. It means visualizing the best version of yourself for your current subordinates. Consider what kind of a leader you want to be for them. Set the goal and begin the continuous improvement. The path to becoming a good leader is an ongoing and endless journey of development. If you achieve being the best, you can always strive to be even better. The journey continues.

Foundations of the best leadership

Many people aspire to become a leader. Some crave it so much that they are willing to do almost anything to achieve it. And that's fine; it's good to have goals. However, what often happens is that when one finally attains a leadership position, the thought process stops there. Very few take the time to contemplate what makes a good leader or how to evolve into one. Once in the role, individuals often just "start leading" and deal with upcoming issues. The beginning can be chaotic, and there is little time to think about leadership styles and its effects on the environment.

Consider whether you want to be the leader that your subordinates remember even ten years from now or for the rest of their lives. Your team members will later reflect on their careers: Who was the best supervisor they had? Will they even remember you at all? Perhaps you treated them poorly, and that's why you left a bad memory. Why wouldn't everyone strive to be good, someone who is remembered for a long time? Why not set the goal to be the **best leader**? Why hesitate to set ambitious goals?

However, the goal is just one part. What are you going to do for becoming a good leader? Regularly dedicating time to contemplate this is crucial. What specific improvements in your actions do you plan to make next? A good approach is to reflect at the end of each workday: what was said, done, how it affected your team members, and would you change anything now? If you notice mistakes, strive to do better in similar situations in the future. Small things matter. Think about the kind of leader you want to be and make the right changes!

Don't try to act as someone else (a proven good leader). Find your own path and be yourself. It's useful to observe how great leaders behave; you can get valuable insights and points from them. However, everyone is unique. Each of us can be an outstanding leader! In this book, I provide you with thoughts to ponder. Implement the ideas that make sense for you. Think critically! Develop your own principles to follow in the future. Keep evolving!

Leadership is challenging. Becoming the best leader is not just about learning a list of things and acquiring certain qualities. A good supervisor should always have situational awareness and tact in various situations, even if a rule "prohibits" a certain way of acting. Set clear goals. Support your team so that they can succeed. Be genuinely interested in your subordinates' careers and their development. Take actions to help them move in the direction they desire in their careers.

This may mean that in the future, they become your colleagues and even exceed you. This can be overwhelming for many supervisors. Good leaders are positive, encouraging, fair, and also take care of themselves.

Common sense

The advices in this book may be contradictory at times. Not all recommendations can be applied to every situation. There is no universally applicable "template" for leadership. That's why leadership is challenging.

Above all the advices and guidelines, common sense and situational awareness should prevail. If something doesn't feel sensible, usually it is not, despite what a textbook might claim. Each situation is different and unique. Proven advice may not necessarily work in all circumstances. Therefore, a sense of situational awareness is essential in every case.

Always start with the common sense. Consider what would be the best course of action at this moment. What does your intuition tell you? Is it conflicting with your leadership principles? Why? The goal is not to overanalyze every situation and paralyze your entire operation. The aim is to act swiftly but also sensibly. If you sense a conflict, it may be appropriate to follow your own "rule book".

Listen the experiences of other leaders. Adopt proven methods from them. You can also learn from their mistakes. Avoid stepping into well-known pitfalls. Everyone makes mistakes, but some of them can be prevented.

The most challenging situations are often unique problem-solving scenarios that cannot be anticipated. Perhaps your logic suggests one thing, and your emotions another. Consider carefully what you do.

What is the best for the individual, the team, and the entire organization? All these considerations may be in conflict.

Reflect on leadership

Think about what kind of a leader you want to be. List the principles that resonate with you and update them as needed. Keep the list easily accessible, such as in a document on your phone. It should be concise and clear. Even if you are already an experienced leader, reflection is a valuable exercise. By observing others and reading books, you can discover new ideas. If it feels challenging to start to write the list, begin by jotting down things you definitely won't do as a leader. You can also use the ideas presented in this book as a basis and supplement them with thoughts that fit best for you.

Set specific goals

Nothing is as frustrating as receiving a long list of goals that are unclear and not prioritized. Firstly, each of them should be SMART. There should be no ambiguity or room for interpretation in the objective. It should be clear what is meant, how the end result can be verified, and within what timeframe it should be accomplished.

Additionally, objectives should be prioritized. Not all tasks hold equal importance. Without prioritization, it's easy for the least significant objectives to be achieved while the most crucial ones are neglected. This is because the easiest tasks to accomplish are typically at the bottom of the priority list.

Moreover, it's not advisable to assign too many objectives to a subordinate at once. Doing so causes unnecessary distress and complicates prioritization. Take enough time yourself to prioritize: What is truly relevant and what is not. Recognize that the world is constantly changing. Is it necessary to review objectives regularly, for instance, every quarter or month? In my opinion, it's absolutely worth considering more frequently than just once a year during performance reviews.

Respect people

It all starts with respecting others, especially your team members. Don't be arrogant towards anyone. You can always learn something new from others, whether it's a new perspective or a different way of working. Keep an open mind.

Good manners are essential in the workplace and in leadership. Be polite and treat others well. Spread kindness. It will come back to you many times over. The above does not mean that you should let others control you. For example, you can argue and be a "tough" leader, but always be courteous and respectful to others.

Of course, there are situations where a leader may lose trust in their subordinate. A team member's behavior can be so inappropriate that its effects are long-lasting – often permanent. For instance, continuous breaking of promises is hard to forgive. Even if you no longer want to have any dealings with them, you often still have to work with them. The situation can become difficult and require reflection on how your dynamics will work in the future. My advice is to remain neutral and professional. Work matters are dealt with together, but you don't have to have more interaction with anyone than necessary if you don't want to.

Be fair

Do not show favoritism towards any of your subordinates or be unfair. Each of your team members should have equal opportunities to succeed. Provide everyone with the same conditions to develop and get their work done. Especially, fairness should be shown in the allocation of your own time towards your subordinates. In practice, this means that you cannot allocate your personal time (such as mentoring) to only a selected few individuals. Not everyone wants attention as much, but it's good to ask them consistently. People need your support and time in different ways. It should be given, but the situation cannot remain unbalanced for long. Leader's personal time can become a source of envy and cause discord if some receive it and others do not.

Different rewards should also be balanced. Publicly rewarding individuals with tangible rewards is not advisable. It immediately triggers envy because, in reality, there are always more people who deserve the reward. Therefore, reward the whole team publicly and exceptional individuals separately in private. The same principles apply to praise. It's different to give positive feedback to the entire team than to individuals. If you publicly speak well of an individual, then praise should come to everyone shortly afterward. Always consider how you make others feel in different situations!

Give your all

Don't make excuses for yourself or others. Give your all to succeed as a leader, achieve your own goals, and ensure that your team members succeed in their work. If it requires shoveling dirt, do it. Don't isolate yourself as a leader and merely issue commands to others. If resources are tight and you can contribute to progress with your own effort, get involved. However, remember, that leadership is always your primary responsibility.

Continuous improvement

Although there's often talk about "overanalyzing" and unnecessary "dwelling" on things, still reflect on past leadership situations. The goal should be improvement and making things better in the future, not dwelling on past mistakes.

Analyze your own actions: Are you constantly making the same mistakes? What are your strengths and weaknesses? Think about special situations and how they could be prevented and handled better in the future. The aim should be continuous improvement on personal, team, and organizational levels. There's always room for improvement because one is never "complete".

Analysis doesn't necessarily have to take up a lot of time. Sometimes, pondering during a coffee break alone is sufficient. Often, it's useful to talk to others.

More important matters can be thought through more carefully. However, it's not advisable to spend one's entire life analyzing mistakes.

Get to know individuals

The better you know your team members, the more likely you are to succeed in leading them. When you understand their strengths, personalities, and working styles, you can lead them more effectively. If your team is entirely new, spend time at the beginning getting to know them. Engage in conversations and ask directly if they're satisfied, what could be improved, and what career aspirations they have. Arrange a joint kick-off where you can also spend time together doing something unrelated to work.

Team members may not be familiar with each other beforehand. So, it's good to get acquainted and do things together. It's also important to have discussions with each individual separately.

Lead each person individually

We are all unique and different. Each person should be led in an individual way. We often behave slightly in a different way depending on the person. Leadership should also be adapted according to who is involved. A novice junior may need more detailed guidance, whereas an experienced expert may not need to be "led" at all. They can work autonomously. However, even experienced individuals often have concerns, although they don't need support in the actual work. It's important to listen to their concerns and do everything possible to improve the situation.

Delegate responsibility

Avoid micromanaging and let professionals do their work undisturbed. Grant them freedoms and responsibilities to decide how they accomplish their tasks. However, keep your finger on the pulse and monitor the situation. If things don't seem to be heading in the right direction, intervene immediately and try to come up with a solution together. People are usually more motivated when they can decide things related to their work themselves. So, involve your team members in planning and decision-making on how to achieve success together.

It's often difficult to gauge the right level of monitoring without slipping into micromanagement. The most important thing for a leader is to help their organization achieve its goals. If you're not sufficiently informed about things, it can be difficult to know where things stand. Conversely, if you're too involved and making decisions on every detail, it kills motivation and innovation.

Be firm but fair

It's not advisable to be a dictator as it stifles the atmosphere. However, firmness is necessary. Yet, there's a fine line as to when leadership becomes too strict. The situation needs constant fine-tuning. If the team is entirely self-directed and efficient, leadership is easy.

Always be fair and equitable. Treat everyone equally. If you're firm, be so with everyone. One of the easiest ways to demotivate someone is to treat them worse than others. Even the smallest things matter. Therefore, ensure that you praise and give recognition to everyone when it's due. Be consistent. Don't treat others unequally. This can sometimes be challenging because each person should be led in their own special way.

Be accessible

Many leaders have client responsibilities or other assigned tasks in addition to leading their own organization. Some think that the client is the number one priority, while others believe that their own team is the most important. As a leader, you must consider the priority order for the organization so that there is enough time to serve everyone.

Serving the client is crucial because often they "pay everyone's salaries". Your task is to interrupt your work when the client calls or visits. Additionally, your team needs you. Strive to help your team in every way possible and remove obstacles to their success. Interrupt your own work when a team member calls or visits – if it is in any means possible. Give your full attention when communicating with someone. The other person should feel that you genuinely care and are interested. Always be helpful.

A leader is usually constantly bombarded with interruptions. You'll have to get used to that. Clients, team members, and other stakeholders constantly interrupt you. However, these should not be seen as disturbances. They are opportunities to serve better. Prioritizing your own task list is challenging for a leader. How to prioritize tasks related to customers, the team, and others? You'll need to adjust your task list constantly. At the end of the book, there are ideas and help for this problem area.

Stay positive

Lead by example and be positive. If you want a good work atmosphere, don't dampen the mood yourself. Of course, you don't need to be overly positive all the time. But the overall vibe should be cheerful and smiles should come easily. Nobody wants to work with negative people. Smiles and good vibes bring joy to the environment and spread positivity.

Always try to see things positively and focus on the good aspects. Never feed into negative spirals or echo negative comments. Negativity spreads like wildfire. It never advances anything. Not all tasks at work are always enjoyable. Still it's not worth complaining about them or encouraging others to do so either. Positivity should also be considered in recruitments too.

Motivation and recognition

Motivation is one of the most important aspects of leadership. Even a single wrong sentence can destroy motivation for a long time. When goals are specific and well-communicated, I recommend to be a **servant leader**. This doesn't mean doing things for your subordinates. Rather, the idea is to be there as to support and to coach, with an open-door policy. When challenges arise, a leader doesn't focus on finding someone to blame but instead focuses on supporting their subordinates. The approach is to ask: What is the situation, and what would be the best way forward from here? What can we learn from this so that we can prevent this problem in the future or better prepare for it?

Motivate

Motivation is undeniably a crucial factor. A motivated team member undoubtedly performs better. Try to think every day about how you can increase everyone's enthusiasm for work. Motivation can be divided into two areas:

1. Eliminate all factors that kill enthusiasm.

2. Increase things that bring positive energy.

Motivation is like trust: it may take a long time to build it, but it can be lost in an instant. One poorly handled situation can completely kill the desire to work. Likewise, think about actions left undone totally.

Always be vigilant and avoid saying or doing the wrong things. Consider what is fair. People are motivated by different things. However, aspects related to demotivation are usually more common than those related to motivation. You can go a long way by being fair, positive, and polite to everyone. The key is to avoid things that diminish motivation. If you can do that, you're already way ahead.

After that, you can focus on things that increase motivation. However, nothing helps if things go wrong in avoiding demotivation. Poor behavior can reduce your employees' enthusiasm to zero. On the other hand, positive actions gradually raise it "few degrees" at a time.

It's often thought that money and various benefits motivate people. It's certainly true that compensation must be at a sufficient level. However, after fulfilling these "basic needs," there's more weight on things that are free or nearly free. These may include pleasant colleagues and atmosphere, sufficient praise, the opportunity to influence one's own tasks and goals, and flexible work and vacation times.

Usually, creatively small things can have a significant impact. For example, giving roses on International Women's Day can be a small and nice gesture. Similarly, if you and your team overcame a difficult situation together, it can weight heavily in the job satisfaction and commitment to the organization. Especially if the leader's actions and behavior were excellent in that situation. This individual may fondly recall this for a long time.

Give feedback

Everyone needs feedback to improve. However, criticism isn't always easy to handle. Ideally, feedback should be given directly so that the recipient sees it as an opportunity to grow – not as negative criticism. Without external information about one's behavior, it's difficult to develop. It takes good self-esteem and self-awareness to notice one's own mistakes. While feedback on the performance should be direct, it's essential to consider the recipient's character. Upsetting someone isn't productive. However, issues shouldn't be swept under the rug either. Even giving direct feedback can be prefaced by talking about continuous improvement. Everyone has strengths and areas for improvement.

Reward and praise

It's always worthwhile to praise subordinates whenever there's even the slightest reason. Even small achievements deserve recognition. There's no reason not to give positive feedback. Everyone feels good when they hear they've done well, come up with a good idea, or achieved something positive. Generally, praise improves motivation. However, avoid excessive praise to prevent it from sounding sarcastic. Colleagues and supervisors also want to hear positive things. Feedback is important for everyone at all levels. We can always strive to improve.

If you have the opportunity to reward good performance, always do so. Even a small reward is better than nothing. In the long run, a good incentive is a salary increase. It's worth holding onto good performers and increasing salaries for consistent high-quality work.

However, it's important to consider that rewarding individual employees may cause jealousy among others. Therefore, I recommend encouraging individuals privately and the entire team collectively. If the majority of the team has performed well, it's often more sensible to reward the whole team.

Delegate and empower

While you should support your team members, they can also support you. Find a sensible boundary for what you delegate to them and what you do yourself. Generally, giving responsibility and authority to others motivates them. Avoid being too controlling and micromanaging. Let team members actually perform tasks in the way they see fit. Monitor the situation and offer support. It's easy to get too involved in a task delegated to someone else. The most important thing is to achieve the goal, not necessarily the path taken to get there.

Your team is fantastic. The power of individuals and the community is strong. People often perform much more challenging tasks than you (or they themselves) might realize. When a challenging task is accomplished, the atmosphere is heavenly. Stepping out of one's comfort zone always leads to growth.

Develop the team

Help yourself and your team to improve - continuously. Unfortunately, not everyone wants this. Nevertheless, fairness should be considered. Everyone should be offered opportunities, even if they don't want to seize them. That's perfectly okay.

Consider various ways to promote team success at both team and individual levels. Development may include self-organized or purchased training and courses, team workshops, retrospectives, or mentoring and coaching. It's worth talking to each individual about how they'd like to develop and then planning together how to proceed in that direction. Remember that the plan must also be implemented, so it doesn't just remain an exercise in theory.

Developing subordinates also involves their career planning. Ask where a subordinate wants to aim. Plan together what prerequisites it would require. Act accordingly. You cannot promise a specific position to anyone in advance. However, you can together seek out education and experience that would make a new job possible.

Recruit effectively

Recruitment is one of the most crucial tasks for a leader. It's essential to constantly strive to improve in this area. Recruitment serves two main purposes: replacing employees who have left and facilitating growth. Even if the team and individuals are generally satisfied, someone will eventually leave. People move, seek change, and depart for various reasons, even if they are content. It's obvious that dissatisfied individuals will leave as soon as they find a better job.

Simply replacing departing employees requires time every year.

Companies want to grow, which usually means that your team needs more people. You might be in a constant recruitment process throughout the year for one or more positions. Therefore, it's advisable to approach hiring positively – it's an integral part of your job description.

Recruitment is a tough game. The rarer the wanted expertise, the harder it is to attract applicants to your team. Sometimes, you may not receive any applications at all. Even if there are applicants, there may not be anyone you'd want to hire. Expect that the recruitment process will consume a lot of your work and calendar time.

It all starts with your company's and your own image. Potential candidates will undoubtedly research how your company presents itself on its website, LinkedIn, in the news, and in the public references. Likewise, they'll check you out. It's essential to make yourself and your company as attractive as possible (while being honest). This requires consistent effort over the years; quick fixes won't help.

Carefully consider the content of your job postings. Try to stand out from the crowd. Most job advertisements follow the same (dull) pattern. When you have a good job posting, push it through every channel, especially on LinkedIn. The more you've networked over the years, the more visibility your job posting will gain.

Always ask for recommendations from your subordinates and friends. Also, go through your own LinkedIn contacts – could there be potential candidates there? This also underscores the importance of long-term work in good leadership: if you've left a positive impression on others, your job offer will surely interest old acquaintances.

Avoid these!

Why are there bad leaders in the world? Based on my own observations, there seem to be a lot of them. Conversely, good leaders seem to be rarely found. This book has gone through the qualities that good leaders possess. Vice versa, bad leaders do not have these qualities.

This section lists some really bad behaviors (partly opposite to what has already been discussed elsewhere in the book). It could be said that if you avoid these behaviors and traits, you're already somewhat on the right track. But that doesn't make you a good leader yet.

All inappropriate behavior is completely unacceptable. This covers all actions contrary to good manners. Yelling has never motivated anyone. Belittling someone or things important to them erodes any remaining respect for the leader. Listening is crucial, so interrupting or talking over others is disrespectful. Any physical misconduct, such as pounding fists on tables or slamming doors, is very immature and only demonstrates a lack of self-control.

Favoritism towards one or a few subordinates over others also falls into bad leadership. Chasing for scapegoats creates a climate of fear and stifles the organization. Continuously bombarding subordinates with new tasks does not motivate anyone. Related to this, lack of prioritization is one of the worst mistakes in leadership. Often, it's wondered why subordinates are not performing. They are often flooded with tasks, and these tasks have not been prioritized. Determining the order of importance is the leader's responsibility. You can't just fill their inbox with everything you want them to do.

Indecision and overly hasty/unthinking decisions somewhat belong to the same category. It's not advisable to make thoughtless decisions, but on the other hand, you can't endlessly ponder over a decision. It's more important to make some sort of decision than no decision at all. You can always reassess the situation if external factors change.

Lastly, there's a more ambiguous category: "unnecessaries." Have you ever (or often) received completely bizarre commands? You can't understand why a particular thing should be done. Maybe you even try to question why it's done or suggest something else (but the command doesn't change). Eventually, you carry out the order, but you're always left wondering why the task was done in the first place.

It's possible that the person issuing the order knows something (that the subordinate doesn't know), and in light of that knowledge, the command makes sense. This is certainly the case in some instances. However, it often comes to mind that aren't things thought through one step further. What are the consequences? Often you can find yourself in a strange situation when you are asked to achieve only one KPI[1] with no matter what it costs. This can mean that many other very important issues are "forgotten".

[1] Key Performance Indicator

Special situations

Leadership is easy when everything is going well. True skills are tested when there are special situations or difficult periods. Exceptional situations can range from one extreme to another. After many years of experience, a leader may believe that she/he encountered all the possible difficulties. This is rarely the case.

Special situations often arise unexpectedly, and the pressure to resolve it or make a decision can be intense. It's always worth considering whether the situation requires immediate action or if it could be pondered for a moment. On the other hand, one cannot avoid making a decision. Rarely the situation is so urgent that actions must be taken immediately (for example, if people were in danger).

Life is diverse, and this is reflected in the workplace. Leisure time events don't always have a direct connection to work life, but still we're all human beings. If something negative happens in our personal life, those things may linger in the mind during work hours and thereby affect the performance. This often creates challenging situations for a leader to ponder.

For example, the death of a subordinate's loved one can be devastating. Support and listening should be provided to the person. However, it's not advisable to take on all the concerns and sorrows of the subordinates. That quickly becomes too heavy to bear. Help is usually available from various sources, both for the subordinate and for the leader: occupational health services, HR, colleagues, mentors, or one's own supervisor. Support should be sought when necessary. No one can be forced to accept help but you can recommend it.

A good rule of thumb is to remain calm and not to get upset. Even if the situation is very difficult and even personal, try to be as objective as possible. Calmness does not mean slowness. Sometimes there are situations in which action needs to be taken very quickly. Occasionally decisions have to be made very quickly, and there's little time for consideration.

If necessary, take a break or sleep on it before making a decision. There are situations in which many questions arise in the leader's head:

• How do we reach the goal?

• How do I take care of my subordinates?

• Am I fair to everyone?

• Am I considering the bigger picture?

• How does this affect the client relationship?

- What are the financial implications for the company (reputation)?

- How does this affect the entire team?

The answers to these questions may be conflicting. So what should you do?

There must be a limit how far you go in "treat people well". Even though you take care of your subordinates, you can't "coddle" them, and fairness must be remembered. Even if you want to be nice to everyone all the time, it may not always be possible. On the other hand, necessary decisions cannot be avoided.

One classic situation is: you have a top individual in your team who achieves great results but doesn't get along with others. Or the person even terrorizes the rest of the team. Should he/she be kept in the group or not? If it's a narcissist or someone who intentionally causes distress in the team, I believe they should be removed. However, situations are not always black and white, so it requires careful investigation and consideration before decisions are made.

Cultural differences can also lead to peculiar situations. They can increase potential misunderstandings and create conflicts that might not otherwise exist. It's the leader's job to find a suitable balance so that each individual can be who they want to be. However, other people should always be considered. Sometimes conflicts are difficult to resolve.

Don't be afraid to apologize

Apologizing and asking for forgiveness is sometimes too rare at work. If something has gone wrong or even possibly gone wrong, a (sincere) apology costs nothing. It can easily prevent a difficult situation from escalating further. I have often apologized at the office, even if I didn't feel that I had done anything wrong. Sometimes I've apologized on behalf of another person or the organization I represent. Someone might ask, why apologize if you haven't done anything wrong? There are situations in which the bigger picture is more important than "being right".

It's not always essential to be right. Sometimes it's best just to defuse the situation to prevent it from worsening. Think a couple of moves ahead in your chess game and consider how different responses will affect the situation. I don't mean that you should take the blame all the time. The point is that a person with good self-esteem sees the bigger picture rather than selfishly focusing only on themselves.

Be prepared for surprises

Things practically never turn out as originally planned. Along the way, we learn new things, people's minds may change, or an external event may disrupt the operating environment. It's wise to mentally prepare for changes and surprises and have good processes in place.

In planning, it's always sensible to agree on the process for reacting to changes (in the environment). A well-agreed and documented way of working in advance significantly facilitates change management. If there is no process or it's hastily agreed upon, there's often a temptation to "cut corners". In practice, there's not enough time to consider what would be a good way to proceed. Changes can also be positive, and in such cases, all the potential should be reached. The process can be light or heavy, but it's worth agreeing on it in advance. In agile methods, changes are continuous.

Surprises may not always be external. You can't always prepare for them with procedures or processes. Nevertheless, be mentally prepared because they always come up.

Address problems immediately

Problems grow larger the longer they exist. Address them immediately when you see one emerging. It is also beneficial to foster an atmosphere where everyone proactively brings challenges to light and collaboratively resolves them without blame. It is advisable to communicate and relay the identified issues to relevant stakeholders as hiding them does not help; they usually surface regardless. The earlier you communicate about a problem, the easier it is to address it. This also cultivates an open atmosphere, alleviating concerns for clients or other stakeholders that something is being concealed. They can trust that issues will be brought to their attention as they arise. Problems can be addressed politely and constructively. Blame does not help. Let's focus on solutions rather than on attributing blame.

Ask for help

If you encounter a problem that you or your team cannot solve independently, it is advisable to seek help promptly. If you have the opportunity to escalate the issue within your organization, do so immediately. It's worth seeking assistance and exploring a wide range of options. This applies to all problems, whether it's delivering a project or responding to an environmental disaster.

Be open

In most situations, full transparency serves as a solid foundation. However, it's crucial to maintain etiquette and politeness at all times. Concealing or delaying matters yields no positive outcomes. Therefore, it's advisable to disclose unpleasant news as soon as possible.

Exaggerating or downplaying issues usually backfires. If there's a problem or negative news, it's essential to follow up by explaining its implications for people. Explain when it occurs, and how to move forward. If there's a solution, share it.

Sometimes there are matters that cannot be disclosed immediately or at all, due to legal or confidentiality reasons. These can be challenging for leaders to handle internally, often leaving them with no one to confide in. For instance, you might be aware that the company needs to initiate restructuring negotiations, but you can't announce it yet. Stay calm and prepare yourserlf for a formal announcement.

Anticipate how to respond if someone asks about the issue directly or indirectly. There might be situations where a leader feels compelled to lie, claiming ignorance about the matter. These can be excruciating for an honest leader who avoids dishonesty. Often, it's possible to navigate such situations by telling the truth. If lying seems the only option, justify it to yourself. Otherwise, your body language and facial micro expressions may easily give you away to an astute observer. When the matter is finally revealed, acknowledge that you couldn't disclose it earlier.

Termination

Sometimes situations arise where it feels like there's only one option: to terminate an employee. It can be an emotionally challenging time for a leader (and, of course, the employee in question). It's crucial to carefully consider whether this is the right course of action or if there are other alternatives.

Firstly, it's important to distinguish between two different situations: when an employee lacks motivation or when she/he lacks skills. If the individual is motivated but lacks necessary skills, one might consider whether training could help. Sometimes this might seem like a long shot, but often it's not. Could it be possible to change job responsibilities or switch positions within the company? This approach often proves fruitful, although it may not always end well.

If, however, the issue lies with the employee's attitude, it's essential to ascertain the root cause. This can vary widely; personal life circumstances, jealousy, or dissatisfaction with salary could all be factors. The real reason can often be uncovered through discussion, although that's not always feasible. Explore whether there's any way to address the issue.

Unfortunately, attitude adjustment isn't always feasible. In such cases, it might be worth considering the least painful path for the employee to continue their employment elsewhere. This approach should be undertaken with utmost care and sensitivity. Receiving termination notice is already an unpleasant experience for anyone. How the situation is communicated and discussed is of paramount importance. There are multiple ways to present the situation.

When you're left behind

Termination is a difficult situation, but more often than not, you'll find yourself being left behind, not the other way around. When your subordinate informs you of their resignation and departure from the company, it can be a challenging time for a leader. Often, it might even be your 'closest deputy,' someone you've personally recruited and trusted. It can feel truly disheartening, triggering a flood of questions and emotions. Why are they leaving, despite all the care and support I've provided in every aspect? The mind can swiftly oscillate from shock to denial, disappointment, and even anger.

I've witnessed and heard stories of terribly mishandled resignation situations. A leader might turn red with anger, berating the subordinate and labeling them a traitor. They might interrogate why the person is leaving, refusing to accept the situation. Some might even resort to emotional pleas, insisting they can't leave because they're irreplaceable. This is not the way to handle it.

I must admit, this has been a challenging aspect for me as well, especially in the early years of my career. It does hurt when you've invested your time in mentoring someone, only to see them leave. It takes a lot of personal growth to handle such situations better.

The most important thing is to change your attitude towards resignations. We don't own anyone. People will leave, even if we do everything right and are the best possible leaders to them. They leave for various reasons: life circumstances change, they seek faster career progression, better benefits, a change of industry, or simply a desire to explore other environments. There might also be such an enticing opportunity that they can't refuse.

However, it's essential to recognize that people often leave because of their supervisor. Nowadays, people demand good leadership, coaching, and mentoring.

Exceptional leaders are sought after. So, when your subordinate leaves (regardless of the stated reason), it's always an opportunity for honest introspection. Was I the reason for their departure? It's worth analyzing the situation: Could something have been done beforehand to prevent their departure? Could my leadership have been better?

Another crucial aspect is handling the situation well. How you behave will significantly impact whether the person might consider returning someday. If you handle the situation poorly, they will never return and may even spread the word about the poor treatment. Remember, you are constantly representing yourself and the company you work for. When you handle the situation positively, it will be remembered.

So, what should you do when someone comes to you and announces their departure? Firstly, listen calmly to what the person has to say without interruption. Often, they'll also explain why they're leaving (at least the polite version). Always respond genuinely that it's sad to hear they're leaving. If you don't show any regret at all, it's quite odd. Still, it is not wise to pretend anything.

Ask if there's anything that can be done? Could we adjust the job to make it more enjoyable? Would a completely new position within the company be meaningful, or is the salary the biggest issue? Sometimes, the person doesn't want to leave, and it might be possible to negotiate. In that case, I think it's worth trying. However, often the decision has already been made, and there's nothing that can be done.

Praise the subordinate and acknowledge the excellent work she/he has done. Of course, you can't lie. If the person is someone you'd like to stay, she/he probably performed exceptionally well. Thank for the time spent together. Also, express your understanding and genuine regret about their departure. Tell them that you'd be happy to provide a reference. Let them know that they don't even need to ask permission about it in the future. The reference is valid for eternity. I believe this is a good gesture. It doesn't cost you anything to be a good person's referee and enhance their future career possibilities.

Also, let them know that you're available if they want to discuss a possible return in the future. If they need someone to talk to about anything, they can always reach out. No matter if that time will come after a week, a month, or ten years.

So, the most important thing is to handle the situation positively from start to finish and leave the other person with a feeling of 'Wow, I thought this resignation would be tough, but it went well!' If the person leaves with a positive feeling, they might return someday. In any case, you're likely to run into them again at some point. They might even become your future supervisor. The world is a small place.

Also, remember to handle all practical matters: final pay and so on. Be present on their last day at the office, offer lunch, and talk about the good times together. Shake hands with a smile.

Continuous development as a leader

Don't rest on your laurels or boast about your past achievements. A good reputation built over ten years can be destroyed in five minutes. Just one wrong sentence can shatter others' perception of you. So always be courteous and considerate of others.

As a leader, it's essential to constantly strive for improvement. Continuous learning enhances your future career prospects and personal growth. It's also gratifying to witness your own development. Tomorrow, you must be a better leader than today.

The world is constantly changing. So are the technologies, industries, people, and processes. When you're enthusiastic about self-improvement, it also helps in leadership. It's wise to be open to different things. Often, good ideas for your work can be found in other fields, literature, and interactions with various people.

I strongly believe in processes and continuous improvement. When there's a well working process in place, it helps to navigate even through the difficult periods. Straightforward rules are beneficial. In this section, I'll provide some ideas and tips on how to handle various matters. The keywords are efficiency and goal achievement. Regarding the former, it's essential to remember that even though you can free-up your time with efficiency, that spare time is usually used for something else. In other words, efficiency may not necessarily create free time to your calendar. However, it does give us more opportunities to decide how we use the available time.

Time management

You can have several perspectives on efficiency and time management. Here, I present my own way of working. It may be partly or entirely self-evident to many of you. Hopefully, you'll get a few tips or ideas on how to improve your own working method.

Everyone should consider their own time management - at work and during leisure time. You never just spend your own time; you almost always spend others' time as well. Especially in a leadership role, you influence the time management of your subordinates (and usually a much broader range of people). It's worth remembering that team members usually obey when they are asked to do something. If you're constantly bombarding them with various requests (without prioritization), they won't have time to do anything else (the real important tasks).

In time management, it's always essential to consider different perspectives: Does this help us to reach the objectives in the long or short term? What is the opportunity cost when I do this task (or instruct my subordinates to do it)? Remember the good old 80/20 rule: 20 percent effort usually yields 80 percent of the results. Is that sufficient? Usually, it is. Very often, we get caught up in bureaucracy and various "trivialities". Those may give a feeling of accomplishment, but it don't actually progress anything. Avoid that. It's worth establishing your own time management system and continuously improving it.

Goals - Keep your eye on the ball

Clarify your goals and prioritize them. Should something be updated? Consider whether doing a task helps you to achieve your goals or not. If the answer is "no" or you're unsure, it's not worth doing it at all. If doing something doesn't help you to reach your goals, then why do it? It sounds obvious but based on my experience, people do a lot of irrelevant things every day.

Someone might criticize, saying, "but there are these other mandatory tasks". Yes, sometimes you have to do certain tasks that don't seem to make any sense. In those cases, consider whether you would skip doing the task or delegate it. In any case, spend as little time on it as possible. I use the **five-minute rule** for such tasks. More on that later.

Reduce

As a leader, you have a significant impact on the time management of many other people. Try to reduce unnecessary activities. Remember your goals. What activities genuinely make you go forward. Consider carefully which tasks (whether self-assigned or delegated from above) you give to your subordinates and how you give them. Focus on clarity. What do you want them to do? What is the desired outcome and its timeline? When giving your subordinates the opportunity to choose their own way to achieve the goal, it also develops them. Remember that all employees have limited working hours. There's no need to crush them with every possible task. Prioritization is essential: which task is the most important one.

Calendar

Many people have their calendars fully packed. Meetings after meetings. If you can even find time for lunch, let alone breaks. Leaders' calendars are often jam-packed because many want to book meetings with them. If your days are filled with meetings from morning till night, when do you actually have time to do your important tasks? For example, to plan sales, prepare presentations, or consider the well-being of your subordinates?

Approach meetings and calls critically. The same principle applies: does this meeting help reaching my goals or not? Unnecessary meetings can be deleted or declined. Does everyone need to participate in this specific meeting? Or would one representative from your organization suffice? This way, you can, for example, take turns to participate with your colleagues or subordinates. This will significantly enhance your work efficiency.

By skipping even one meeting a day, you save five hours a week for your important tasks. A proven method is to schedule a one-hour private reservation for your lunch break every weekday. Just that gives you a moment to catch your breath during the day. Even more effective is to add another one-hour private event each day. In that slot you can work on your critical tasks. This way, your calendar doesn't fill up automatically every day. You have time to accomplish much more.

I personally prefer having one shared calendar for work and leisure. This way, all events are in one place. After all, we don't have "two lives" so that we could be in two places at the same time. In my work calendar, I include all the events and meetings, even those related to leisure time.

Email management

Emails are surprisingly time consuming for all of us. We receive enormous amounts of emails every day. Therefore, it's important to have good practices for email management. Here are my tips:

1. Consider whether you need to respond to the email you received at all. If not, don't reply. Every email you write, even a short one, takes your time.

2. Note that usually, every email you send will receive a response. This will again take your time (you have to read it and maybe reply). So, try to minimize the number of outgoing emails. A phone call or chat achieves the same thing faster.

3. Write short and concise emails. Nobody has the patience to read novels. If you want to provide a lot of background material, include them as links.

4. Allocate specific times for yourself to keep the email program open. It's not wise to scan and read the emails all the time. Incoming messages interrupt your work. If something is genuinely urgent, they'll call you. The time for reading emails should generally be in the afternoon. The morning is the

best time to produce text and prepare important matters.

5. Turn off all notifications on your laptop and especially on your phone. They interrupt your work and cause constant task switching.

6. Create folders and automatic rules for incoming emails. All "FYI" messages should be moved to a low priority (or similar) folder immediately. Automate as much as possible. This way a lot of "unnecessary" emails goes to a folder that you check maybe once a day or a week.

7. Keep your inbox empty. When the previous point is thoroughly done, your inbox stays better under control. I only have unread and action-required emails in there. I move other emails (if they haven't already been moved) to folders right away. This

way, the amount of emails in the inbox directly correlates with my workload.

8. How to create an effective to-do list? Related to the previous point, the messages in my inbox require some action from me (or are unread). In addition, I keep a task list in my email program. Every task has a deadline. I can also create a schedule for the important emails. This way, I can always see when the next deadline is approaching and prioritize my tasks. All items requiring action are in my email program (either as messages in the inbox or on the task list). If I come up with a new task or receive it, for example, from a phone call, I enter it into the task list.

Substitutes

When you're on vacation or away from work, be genuinely away. Get a substitute even for short absences and let people know about it by using an out-of-office message. Turn off all notifications. Don't check your work emails, Teams, or any other applications. The substitute's task is to handle ongoing matters. No organization should rely solely on any individual. It's poor organizing and management. The cemetery is full of irreplaceable people.

For the substitute, it's a great opportunity to develop and practice leadership skills (or the work of a higher-ranking leader/colleague). So, if you want to advance within the organization, always express your willingness to substitute! Go through what tasks need to be handled during the absence, what can be expected, and what to do if something unexpected happens. I don't recommend that every time an unexpected situation arises, you contact the person being substituted. Otherwise, the person's vacation will never be a real holiday. However, it's worth assessing the situation on a case-by-case basis. Usually, support can be found from higher management or neighboring units.

There can be such serious situations that it's necessary to contact the person being substituted. Nevertheless, it's advisable to agree on some ground rules. For example, one time slot per week for a quick phone call to go through all the issues (as opposed to calling separately for each issue).

The Five-Minute Rule

I've applied a **five-minute rule** to "mandatory" but, in my opinion, unnecessary tasks: If you must do it, spend five minutes on it. No more. These tasks include those that don't genuinely contribute to achieving your goals but must be done for some reason. Often, the five minutes suffices, and no one asks for more. If it's not enough, you can use another five minutes slot and see what happens.

As discussed in previous paragraphs, everyone seems to be in a hurry, yet people spend their time on peculiar things that don't actually matter for achieving their goals. The "feeling" of busyness creates an unreal sense of being an "important" member of the work community. However, that's just not the case. Do the right things efficiently, not the wrong things.

Taking care of yourself

You can't last long if you don't take care of yourself. Aim for eight hours of sleep each night. Try to maintain a regular sleep schedule — this has been proven to have profoundly positive effects on one's life. Even a slight lack of sleep affects your performance immediately and in the long term. There are several excellent books available that delve deeper into the effects of sleep.

Eat regularly, sufficiently, and healthily (but not excessively). You need protein, vegetables, berries, and fruits. For aerobic exercise, you also need carbohydrates. Avoid excessive caffeine, especially in the afternoon. It's advisable not to consume coffee in the evening at all. Consume only little alcohol or skip it totally. Your body doesn't need alcohol for anything. Even small amounts of caffeine and alcohol negatively affect the quality of your sleep. This, in turn, affects other aspects of your life negatively.

In addition to sleep and a healthy diet, good physical fitness helps you cope with demanding work. It's beneficial to engage in diverse forms of exercise, both aerobic and anaerobic. As you get older, muscle mass begins to decline, so anaerobic muscle training is beneficial. It's essential to remember muscle maintenance too. Stretching should be practiced every day, especially after physical activities. Massage can help with tense shoulders or other muscles. Adequate rest is also necessary. Excessive and continuous strenuous training is also harmful. Sufficient recovery days are essential.

Consult a doctor if you're concerned about your health situation. You are responsible for yourself and your health. You cannot outsource it to others. Doctors can provide assistance and advice. I am not a doctor or a nutritionist, so I'm sharing things that have worked for me in my current life situation. It's worth trying and considering what rhythm works best for you. Nevertheless, routines are important. It's worth considering whether they can be modified or improved.

I have personally used a method called the "**forbidden list**". I originally learned it from my close friend and modified it slightly. The idea is to list foods or drinks that are not allowed at all. Precise yes/no lists work for many people. If something is not allowed at all, then even a small bite should be avoided.

Always remember the big picture and your goals. If it's important for you to handle, for example, a demanding business trip where you're presenting, then the priority is to handle that task well. If it absolutely requires unhealthy eating (which I doubt), then do so. Just make sure to get back on track immediately afterward.

Create your own brand

It's advisable to start building your personal (work) brand early in your career. Especially in a leadership role, it has a significant impact on many things. Firstly, it demonstrates activity and diligence, likely improving your career prospects. It probably also affects your interactions with clients or team members.

LinkedIn is undoubtedly the most important tool for building a brand in the workplace. Your profile must be in good shape, and you should add all positive work and education-related aspects, such as job responsibilities and their contents. Simply listing titles won't help outsiders understand what you've actually done or achieved in different positions. Avoid writing too much, but definitely indicate the content, responsibilities, and achievements of each job. All training, courses, and certifications should be included.

Choosing the right picture is crucial: if you're already a leader or aspiring to be one, add a business photo where you're smiling and your head fills most of the picture. You should be recognizable in it. Do not use a ten-year-old photo. Carefully consider your profile description. It's a good idea to list your key skills, interests, and achievements.

Once the profile is polished (and it should be updated whenever you gain more experience), it's essential to focus on actual activities. Showing activity is worthwhile. Liking and commenting on other people's posts is the easiest way to start, but it's not enough. Consider the kind of posts you want to be known for. Even if writing seems difficult, start practicing.

I see leaders bringing forth ideas and writing about "substance" on LinkedIn. Don't write too much, and not on topics that don't interest anyone. I recommend sticking to work-related matters. For example, if you're familiar with a specific industry, technology, or method, you can start by commenting on it or writing a blog.

It's advisable to be registered on the most popular social media platforms. Visit them at least weekly to read about news, even if you don't produce content yourself. There's a lot of information available on social media platforms. People express their opinions and comment issues. Organizations also have their own accounts, and most are active. Someone might ask if the information in social media is always useful. Not necessarily. But by following the posts of your subordinates and clients, you can deepen your knowledge of them.

Change management and communication

Leadership is widely known to involve a lot of communication and interaction. An idea may seem good in your own mind, but if it's not effectively communicated, the situation can end in disaster. In this section, I've divided the matter as follows: by communication, I mean promoting certain things through various channels to a larger audience (as opposed to one individual). By interaction, I mean verbal communication with one person or a small group in a specific situation. Communication skills have been discussed from various perspectives in earlier sections of this book.

Change management is communication, which is why I want to address the topic separately. So, we want to influence people's behavior. Communication may also serve merely an informative purpose: we want the public to know about Issue X (FYI[2]). It's usually more straightforward, so let's focus more on change management.

When aiming for change, it always requires willpower. The larger the issue, the more force is needed. People often inherently resist. For some, it's internal, and it's

---

[2] For Your Information

not externally expressed. Resistance can be strong, and changing it requires persistent effort.

External resistance is visible and loud. Certain individuals adopt more easily a critical attitude and bring up reasons why the change should not be made. Sometimes the game is dirty, and arguments are made with irrelevant matters. Often with scare tactics. It's easy to throw out a general threat that induces fear in people. It can be difficult to dispel once felt, easily disrupting concentration.

In leadership, the message should be as clear and straightforward as possible. Why is this change being made? What does this mean for us as an organization? What does this mean for an individual? What are the steps to be taken and why? What is the timeline? When communication is clear and targeted, it usually works best. After that, the message should be repeated many times and consistently.

Poor leaders seem to have a misconception about change management. They tell about the becoming changes once and assume that a lot will happen overnight. However, in real life, nothing happens yet. No one likely does anything. Change should be prepared before it is communicated to a large audience. First, ensure that there are enough positive change agents to support you. They can be other leaders and/or team members. Once you've got some people on board and excited, it can make leading a larger group easier.

In change management, it's advisable to start from the end (= the desired outcome) and "walk" the path backward. If you want a specific action, consider what concrete steps are needed to achieve it. What needs to happen before each event. If leadership lacks concrete actions to move forward, nothing happens. **Goals cannot be led; actions can**. Even though you plan for change in advance, you'll likely have to agilely adjust something along the way. Not everything will surely go as originally expected. When that happens, reconsider the situation and think about how to proceed in light of the new information.

Presentation skills

A good leader doesn't necessarily have to be the world's best performer. However, having presentation skills and delivering inspiring presentations can facilitate the advancement of many things. This goes especially in change management. I have seen several excellent introverted or even somewhat shy leaders. They usually possess a naturally important skill: listening. If large presentation situations are daunting, don't worry: the most important thing is one-on-one interactions with subordinates.

Preparation for public speaking

Since leaders often face various speaking situations, these skills should be consciously practiced throughout one's career. Even if it seems difficult or even unpleasant, it's worthwhile to start with the basics, such as good preparation. First and foremost, this includes defining the **objective**: what is the essential point of this presentation, what do you want to achieve? It could be, for example, promoting a specific change, educating, motivating, or informing.

Once the objective is clear, you can focus on considering how to best achieve it. An essential part of public speaking is understanding the target audience. This sets the foundation for the entire content of the presentation. It's a different situation to speak to experts in a certain field about a topic they know well than to a general audience that likely has little knowledge of the subject.

Therefore, if possible, find out in advance who will be in your audience. The better you know them and their backgrounds, the better you can plan the level of your message. It's not always possible to know anything about the audience in advance. Also the audience may include people with varying levels of expertise. In such cases, it's difficult to maintain people's interest and motivation throughout the presentation. Consider how you can address different groups or individuals within the audience while keeping the presentation engaging. This may not be easy.

After considering how to achieve your goal, outline the flow of your presentation. How much time do you have? It's usually wise to leave some flexibility for unexpected situations or questions. Listing and outlining the agenda can be a good start to planning the structure of the presentation. There are two different schools of thought on this, but most often it's recommended to start by informing the audience about what the presentation will contain. Go through the agenda; it helps pace the program.

Regarding slides, less is more. Don't make a hundred slides, preferably ten. Also, avoid including too much text on them. Often people design their presentations as "hand-outs" to be shared afterward. However, I don't think this is a good approach. The presentation is a presentation, and its fluency is paramount. The distributed version can be edited later if necessary.

Usually, when you show a slide, the audience starts reading it. If it contains a lot of text, they probably won't be able to listen to your speech attentively at the same time. Therefore, it's better to use less text. Instead, use many images or even short videos. The more you vary the content (text, images, videos), the more engaging your presentation is likely to be. You can even occasionally put a single word or sentence on a slide to prompt interest.

Consider copyright and possible trade secrets in material design. People take pictures with their phones, and presentations are usually shared afterward. Therefore, don't include anything you don't want the whole world to know. Keep such things only in your speech (which also spreads, of course).

However, the most important thing in planning is: start early. Never leave making the presentation to the last day. Start preparing as soon as you know about your next speaking event. Make the first considerations and some notes immediately. Your brain starts working, and your subconscious mind also works when you sleep or do other things. It's best to continue working on the presentation steadily. A week before the presentation, it should be 90% ready.

Allocate time for practice. There are several advantages: when you speak your presentation aloud, you get an idea of its length. In all likelihood, the program progresses slower (or sometimes faster) in a real situation than you estimated. At the same time, speaking aloud helps you hear if some expression you're using is too unusual or inappropriate. At least 3-5 practice sessions are a minimum if you want a smooth presentation. In this respect, people are, of course, different. It's best to present it to someone else at least once. To someone who can comment and ask questions that the audience is likely to ask. Practice, practice, practice.

Remember that your (last) presentation always affects to your reputation! You have probably seen several different presentations, some of which are boring and some poorly made. What kind of impression do you want to give? A good presentation will surely bring positive things to you in the future. Whether your audience is your team, your clients, your partners, or the leadership team of your own company.

If it's possible to check the presentation location in advance, do it. Test the functionality of the equipment. Walk on the stage and give your show once. You gain a psychological advantage when you've already "experienced" the presentation and taken control of the space. Think in advance about what to do if none of the equipment works or other technical problems arise. Also, prepare for other special situations. What if the audience is completely silent? What if there's one challenger in the audience who keeps interrupting?

What if there are many questions? When you're prepared, you don't have to think about everything ad-hoc in the situation.

Tips for public speaking

Always arrive on time, preferably 30-60 minutes before the actual presentation begins. This way, you have time to calm down and relax a bit. The worst thing is to arrive in a terrible rush and barely make it. When you arrive early, you have time to check the venue and equipment. Perhaps you want to take a moment to reflect on and recall the main points of your presentation. It's beneficial to put yourself in a positive mindset. For some, it helps to go to the bathroom just before the presentation, throw your hands up in the air like a winner, and shout "yeah!" For others, recalling a good memory helps. In any case, aim for a positive vibe and a smile.

If there's a coffee break or another networking opportunity before your speaking slot, take advantage of it. Approach people confidently and start conversations. This way, the listeners are already more familiar, and you learn a bit more about them.

It's often a good idea to start the presentation with a brief introduction. Then, engage the audience in some way. For example, you can ask a question related to the topic: "How many of you have..." This way, you're likely to get at least some of the audience to raise their hands. Another classic (and in my opinion, good) way is to ask everyone to stand up. Then, ask a specific group to sit down (e.g., "Sit down if you've never used a co-pilot"). Then, clarify with a new request. However, consider the point of this, so that those who remain standing are not embarrassed (e.g., those who have never done something "cool"). Once the audience is somewhat engaged, they are usually more interested throughout your presentation. Engagement can also be done during the presentation or at the end.

If there are multiple speakers at the same event, it can be good to refer to a point made by the previous speaker that supports your own presentation. This is especially useful if the contents are related.

Consider in advance whether you allow questions during the presentation or only at the end. You can decide the placement based on what feels most natural to you. At the beginning, let the audience know at which time questions are allowed. I usually prefer to allow interruptions. This fosters good dialogue with the audience and adds some unpredictability. The parking lot technique is also handy: write the questions (or have your assistant write them) on post-it notes and stick them on a flip chart for later reference at the end of the presentation.

It's self-evident that you shouldn't speak in a monotone voice. Vary the pitch, speed, and liven up your presentation in other ways. You don't need to exaggerate, but at least don't stand still and speak quietly all the time. Movement on stage, use of hands, changing vocal tones, help keep the audience awake and interested.

Maintain eye contact with the audience at all times. With your eyes and body direction, you can cover all "sectors". A good technique is to establish eye contact with someone on one side and then shift your gaze in the opposite direction while speaking. If staring into people's eyes feels too difficult or nerve-wracking, you can look at the hairline of those in the back row or slightly beyond. This makes it look like you're speaking to everyone.

I prefer the classic "three points" at the end of the presentation. Summarize the most important things because the closing words of the presentation may be the only things some listeners remember.

A good way is to thank the audience and tell them they can contact you afterward, and you're happy to discuss further. It's often convenient to have someone taking notes during your presentation. They jot down all the questions and observe the audience's mood. They tell you which comments work well and which don't. This way, you can get good feedback from a "familiar" person. On the other hand, you don't have to remember or spend your time writing questions and notes. You can focus on delivering the presentation itself. Using a "support person" isn't always possible, but from the perspective of feedback and improvement, it's a really good way to improve as a presenter.

Handling special situations during a presentation

No matter how well you prepare for a presentation or how experienced you are as a speaker, things don't always go according to plan. There are various special situations that can arise, and not all of them can be fully anticipated. It's a good idea to think in advance about a general course of action, no matter what happens. One such approach (not necessarily the best) is to say that you will cover the issue at the end. This way, you may have more ease to conclude your presentation. Let's go through some of the most common special situations.

People who ask or interrupt a lot can be really stressful during your presentation. Some persons always need to show off or undermine others. Some audience people may shout remarks like "that's not true". Often, they have no substantial argument to support their comment. You can ask for clarification from them: can they justify? At worst, your entire presentation time is consumed by such arguments. This isn't beneficial for anyone.

One way is to say that you'll address the final questions and comments at the end of the presentation. If this doesn't help either, the situation is really challenging. It depends, of course, on the type of event and your relationship with the audience. Try to calm the situation. Pause and smile.

Another somewhat differently challenging situation is a completely silent audience. Especially if you were hoping for an interactive crowd that would comment when you ask them questions. In any case, this is ultimately an easier situation than interrupters. In this case, it's best to just continue your presentation normally until the end. Even if you feel like the presentation wasn't successful, it may feel completely different to the audience.

What if the equipment doesn't work? Can you carry on with the show without the support of slides? It's always a good idea to have notes or written small cards with you just in case. Just knowing that there's a backup plan can provide you better confidence. Device issues are rare but that can happen. It's best to rehearse your presentation so well that you don't need slides at all. I've also seen many excellent presentations in which no visual aids were used: it's just pure speech without cue cards. Try to give it a shot: give a presentation without any supporting material.

Keep calm and move on. No matter what unexpected happens, your task is still to carry your presentation through to the end. It may be that this day isn't your best. You may have slept poorly, just recovered from a flu, or had an argument with a loved one. All of these can affect your energy levels and, consequently, be directly or indirectly reflected in your performance. Even though it's difficult, try to shake off at least the negative feelings before your presentation.

Follow-up

Once the presentation is over, consider how you'll handle the post-presentation work. If you've agreed to send materials to the audience, do so promptly. Similarly, if you've promised to answer questions that couldn't be addressed during the event, do it quickly. It goes without saying that you should do everything you've promised. A nice gesture is also to thank the participants. Consider whether to send a personal thank-you to each participant (via private email) or if a collective message to everyone would be more suitable. A personal message will certainly be well-received. The impression left by presentations is always subjective and plays on perceptions. If your post-presentation work can enhance a positive impression, it will surely help in your career later on or open up other opportunities.

Ask for feedback on your presentation and how it could be improved. Evaluate yourself: was there any mistakes, poor word choices, or did you notice the audience dozing off during a certain section? What could be done better next time? Feedback from listeners is of paramount importance. However, remember that you may receive completely contradictory feedback on the same presentation. You can't directly alter your presentation based on a single comment. Take feedback seriously, but always consider which changes are feasible.

If the presentation didn't go perfectly in your opinion or if you made mistakes, don't fret. Mistakes happen to everyone, and they provide learning opportunities. Mistakes are likely to occur in every presentation, and not everything always goes as planned. The main thing is that the audience has largely been satisfied. Don't be discouraged even if the presentation went completely awry. Learn, improve, and start preparing for the next presentation!

Career reflections

No matter how carefully one plans their career path, things don't always go according to expectations, and unexpected situations arise. Start by pondering your goal: what do you aim to achieve? Do you aspire to be the CEO of a publicly traded company, or is leading a single team your dream? It's also wise to regularly reassess (at least annually) whether your feelings on the future has changed.

Sometimes, one's "hunger" for success may grow. While at other times, the thought may arise that the current situation is satisfactory. When thinking about your goal, it's essential to know what is your passion. Without it, it's challenging to sustain years in the same position. However, even though passion is crucial, life's other realities may intervene. It's not always financially or otherwise feasible to pursue what one truly desires. Nevertheless, it's important to consider what feels like the best decision.

In any case, without a goal, it's challenging to identify the factors that contribute to success. Ponder from the end to the beginning what skills are required. In any case, gather useful and desirable experiences and list them on your LinkedIn profile and CV. The more diverse your experience, the broader your opportunity to apply for various positions in the future. It's always wise to possess at least one "real" and sought-after skill, even if your main focus is on leadership (or something else). There is usually more demand for real "doers" than for "small talkers" (who don't actually do much).

A classic consideration is whether it's better to work long for one (or a few) company or to have several shorter jobs. It is not easy to say. Long job periods indicate commitment and accumulation of experience in a specific area. However, multiple job roles and employers can broaden perspectives and provide broader (but perhaps narrower) experience in various areas. Perhaps a certain combination of long and short tenures may be optimal for many.

Another classic consideration concerns expertise. Do you want to specialize in a narrow field or become more of a generalist, knowing a little about a wide range of subjects? Both have their pros and cons: as a specialist, you may be highly sought after and well-paid. However, if the demand for your expertise diminishes, you may find yourself in a difficult situation. You might have to start from the scratch to learn something new or exploring other options. A generalist may find work across a broader spectrum, but the competition is fierce. Paycheck may also be lower due to a higher number of competitors, which could drive compensation down.

The third classic question is: Should you accept unpleasant tasks? Or should you choose those that are more meaningful and feel more aligned with your goals? Decisions can go wrong and not necessarily propel your career forward. Not everything can always be taken into account.

However, the fact remains that someone has to do those unpleasant tasks. But is the job something that no one should do at all? If you gain a reputation for eagerly taking on unpleasant and challenging tasks, this will surely be remembered later on. People are always looking for individuals who take action and don't complain at every turn. Even leaders seek can-do people, not complainers.

It should always be remembered that one's well-being must be taken care of. If certain tasks are genuinely too mentally taxing, it's not worth doing them. On the other hand, we often underestimate ourselves. I recommend being generally open-minded to offered tasks and saying "yes" more than "no". Often, you learn a lot and develop yourself as a professional from these challenging tasks.

Becoming the best leader?

Will you become the best leader by following the ideas in this book? You will certainly become better and continuously seek to improve. The most important thing is to reflect on your actions. What kind of a leader do you want to be? How can you apply the teachings in a way that suits your situation? Find your own way and develop yourself.

One of the most crucial skills is the situational awareness. It can't be learned from a book. You must notice situations that require flexibility. Not all rules can be applied to every situation. Put yourself in another person's shoes and consider the best solution. Without empathy, one cannot succeed. People deserve respect.

Precise goals are the basis for progress. In addition, prioritization is needed: what is the most important if there isn't time for everything? Goals cannot be managed on their own. Consider what actions are needed to achieve and manage them. Support from a supervisor is especially important. However, avoid micromanaging.

Invest in motivating and rewarding people. Satisfied subordinates achieve better results and have can-do attitude. Hold on to good people. Reward them appropriately. Remember good principles for praising individuals and teams. Always maintain a positive attitude and view changes as opportunities!

Prepare for surprises. Life is diverse, and it reflects to the workplace. Address problems immediately. If you don't react to challenging situations, you tacitly approve them. Seek help if necessary. Remember to take care of yourself as well. The work of a leader is demanding, and it cannot be sustained for long without enough sleep or a healthy diet.

Boldly start practicing leadership. Seize opportunities to develop. However, remember that situations are real to people. If you treat them poorly, it will be remembered for a long time. The effects of bad decisions are long-lasting. It's easier to break things than to fix them. Build trust persistently. There are too many bad leaders in the world — make yourself the best!

About the author

Jari Niemi has worked in the IT industry for over 20 years, including 12+ years in leadership positions. With a background of two Master of Science degrees (Technology and Economics), he has led teams and units up to 90 people. Jari enjoys spending time with the family, exercising, reading, writing, and traveling.

Mentoring and coaching younger professionals in the field of leadership is close to his heart. Sharing openly experiences and training new leaders is rewarding for both parties. Helping others to advance their careers should be on the agenda of all professionals. No one is ever fully ready as a leader - there is always room for improvement!